If you have purchased this Diary/Journal without its cover, it may be a stolen book. Neither the publisher or the author is under any obligation to provide professional services in anyway, legal, health or in any form which is related to this book, its contents advice or otherwise.

The law and practices vary from country to country and state to state.

If legal or professional information is required, the purchaser, or the reader should seek the information privately and best suited to their particular needs, and circumstances.

The author and publisher specifically disclaim any liability that may be incurred from the information within this book.

All rights reserved. No part of this Diary/Journal, including the interior design, images, cover design, diagrams, or any intellectual property (IP), icons and photographs may be reproduced or transmitted in any form by any means (electronic, photocopying, recording or otherwise) without the prior permission of the publisher. ©

Copyright© 2023 MSI Australia

All rights reserved.

ISBN: 978-0-6459680-1-9

Published by How2Books
Under licence from MSI Ltd, Australia
Company Registration No: 96963518255
NSW, Australia

See our website: www.how2books.com.au
Or contact by email: sales@how2books.com.au
Covers and Copyright owned by MSI, Australia

MSI acknowledges the author and images, text and photographs used in this book.

Published by How2Books

10% of the sale of each book helps to support Diabetes Type One and Cancer Research.

THE FLOWER ARRANGERS

DIARY 2024

The use of space in any floral design is equally as important as the flowers and foliage used.

JANUARY

1)	Sunday
2)	Monday
3)	Tuesday
4)	Wednesday

JANUARY

5)	Thursday
6)	Friday
7)	Saturday
8)	Sunday

JANUARY

9) Monday

10) Tuesday

11) Wednesday

12) Thursday

JANUARY

13) Friday

14) Saturday

15) Sunday

16) Monday

JANUARY

17) Tuesday

18) Wednesday

19) Thursday

20) Friday

JANUARY

21)	Saturday
22)	Sunday
23)	Monday
24)	Tuesday

JANUARY

25)	Wednesday
26)	Thursday
27)	Friday
28)	Saturday

JANUARY

29) Sunday

30) Monday

31) Tuesday

Your Notes
....
....
....
....

Not all flower arrangements need to be created on oasis, careful placement and stem-length cutting can lead to incredible floral arrangement displays...

FEBRUARY

1)	Wednesday
2)	Thursday
3)	Friday
4)	Saturday

FEBRUARY

5) Sunday

6) Monday

7) Tuesday

8) Wednesday

FEBRUARY

9)	Thursday
10)	Friday
11)	Saturday
12)	Sunday

FEBRUARY

13) Monday

14) Tuesday

15) Wednesday

16) Thursday

FEBRUARY

17)	Friday
18)	Saturday
19)	Sunday
20)	Monday

FEBRUARY

21) Tuesday
22) Wednesday
23) Thursday
24) Friday

FEBRUARY

25)	Saturday
26)	Sunday
27)	Monday
28)	Tuesday

Your Notes

....
....
....
....

A semi-crescent floral design takes precision and practice, but once accomplished can lead to creative designs of interest.

MARCH

1)	Wednesday	
2)	Thursday	
3)	Friday	
4)	Saturday	

MARCH

5)	Sunday
6)	Monday
7)	Tuesday
8)	Wednesday

MARCH

9)	Thursday
10)	Friday
11)	Saturday
12)	Sunday

MARCH

| 13) Monday |
| 14) Tuesday |
| 15) Wednesday |
| 16) Thursday |

MARCH

17)	Friday

18)	Saturday

19)	Sunday

20)	Monday

MARCH

21) Tuesday

22) Wednesday

23) Thursday

24) Friday

MARCH

25) Saturday
26) Sunday
27) Monday
28) Tuesday

MARCH

29)	Wednesday
30)	Thursday
31)	Friday

Your Notes

....
....
....
....

Blocking of colour is important for visual impact and balance of the visual materials used.

In the above, column stock adds the heaviness, while the individual stock flowers are indeed light in appearance. The soft shapes of the roses, add to the flat planes of the cream lilies in the first placements.

APRIL

1) Saturday

2) Sunday

3) Monday

4) Tuesday

APRIL

5) Wednesday

6) Thursday

7) Friday

8) Saturday

APRIL

9)	Sunday

10)	Monday

11)	Tuesday

12)	Wednesday

APRIL

13) Thursday

14) Friday

15) Saturday

16) Sunday

APRIL

17) Monday

18) Tuesday

19) Wednesday

20) Thursday

APRIL

21) Friday

22) Saturday

23) Sunday

24) Monday

APRIL

25)	Tuesday
26)	Wednesday
27)	Thursday
28)	Friday

APRIL

29)	Saturday
30)	Sunday

Your Notes

....
....
....
....
....
....
....
....
....

Using limited numbers of flowers can add elegance and interest to simple but stylish flower designs.

With just five Dutch iris, two lily flowers and the careful placement of foliage on a mirror base adds to the magic of the design.

MAY

1)	Monday	
2)	Tuesday	
3)	Wednesday	
4)	Thursday	

MAY

5)	Friday
6)	Saturday
7)	Sunday
8)	Monday

MAY

9)	Tuesday
10)	Wednesday
11)	Thursday
12)	Friday

MAY

13)	Saturday
14)	Sunday
15)	Monday
16)	Tuesday

MAY

17)	Wednesday
18)	Thursday
19)	Friday
20)	Saturday

MAY

| 21) Sunday |
| 22) Monday |
| 23) Tuesday |
| 24) Wednesday |

MAY

25) Thursday
26) Friday
27) Saturday
28) Sunday

MAY

29)	Monday
30)	Tuesday
31)	Wednesday

Your Notes
....
....
....
....
....

You can always enhance your floral work by adding fruits and vegetables or by using different coloured and shaped leaves.

JUNE

1)	Thursday
2)	Friday
3)	Saturday
4)	Sunday

JUNE

5)	Monday
6)	Tuesday
7)	Wednesday
8)	Thursday

JUNE

9)	Friday
10)	Saturday
11)	Sunday
12)	Monday

JUNE

13)	Tuesday

14)	Wednesday

15)	Thursday

16)	Friday

JUNE

17)	Saturday
18)	Sunday
19)	Monday
20)	Tuesday

JUNE

21)	Wednesday
22)	Thursday
23)	Friday
24)	Saturday

JUNE

25) Sunday

26) Monday

27) Tuesday

28) Wednesday

JUNE

29)	Thursday

30)	Friday

Your Notes

....
....
....
....
....
....
....
....
....
....

With bright sunflowers in the above arrangement, extra interest is added by the mandarines added, on skewers, in the larger arrangement, and then the colour is extended to the extra placement of the frut in the bowl beside the main design. To add warmth to any design, you can add a lighted candle or safer, use a battery powered candle to enhance the creative appearance of the design.

JULY

1)	Saturday
2)	Sunday
3)	Monday
4)	Tuesday

JULY

5)	Wednesday
6)	Thursday
7)	Friday
8)	Saturday

JULY

9) Sunday

10) Monday

11) Tuesday

12) Wednesday

JULY

13) Thursday

14) Friday

15) Saturday

16) Sunday

JULY

17)	Monday
18)	Tuesday
19)	Wednesday
20)	Thursday

JULY

21) Friday

22) Saturday

23) Sunday

24) Monday

JULY

25)	Tuesday
26)	Wednesday
27)	Thursday
28)	Friday

JULY

29)	Saturday
30)	Sunday
31)	Monday

Your Notes
....
....
....
....
....

Using a combination of white and yellow, is both refreshing and interesting in the above design. The lemons are cleverly hiding the mechanics that at keeping the placements firm and in place.

AUGUST

1)	Tuesday
2)	Wednesday
3)	Thursday
4)	Friday

AUGUST

5)	Saturday
6)	Sunday
7)	Monday
8)	Tuesday

AUGUST

9)	Wednesday
10)	Thursday
11)	Friday
12)	Saturday

AUGUST

13)	Sunday
14)	Monday
15)	Tuesday
16)	Wednesday

AUGUST

17)	Thursday
18)	Friday
19)	Saturday
20)	Sunday

AUGUST

21)	Monday
22)	Tuesday
23)	Wednesday
24)	Thursday

AUGUST

25) Friday

26) Saturday

27) Sunday

28) Monday

AUGUST

29)	Tuesday

30)	Wednesday

31)	Thursday

Your Notes

....
....
....
....

Using embellishments in your creative designs can add romance and character. In the above example, I have added the strings of pearls, lighted candles which are sitting on a mirror base.

SEPTEMBER

5) Tuesday

6) Wednesday

7) Thursday

8) Friday

SEPTEMBER

5)	Tuesday
6)	Wednesday
7)	Thursday
8)	Friday

SEPTEMBER

9)	Saturday
10)	Sunday
11)	Monday
12)	Tuesday

SEPTEMBER

13)	Wednesday
14)	Thursday
15)	Friday
16)	Saturday

SEPTEMBER

17)	Sunday
18)	Monday
19)	Tuesday
20)	Wednesday

SEPTEMBER

21) Thursday

22) Friday

23) Saturday

24) Sunday

SEPTEMBER

25)	Monday
26)	Tuesday
27)	Wednesday
28)	Thursday

SEPTEMBER

29)	Friday
30)	Saturday

Your Notes
....
....
....
....
....
....
....
....
....
....

With planning and precision, an effective floral design can be made from just two flowers, as seen in the above. Visual space is created by cleverly using the green spear grass in precise placements.

OCTOBER

1)	Sunday
2)	Monday
3)	Tuesday
4)	Wednesday

OCTOBER

5)	Thursday
6)	Friday
7)	Saturday
8)	Sunday

OCTOBER

9) Monday

10) Tuesday

11) Wednesday

12) Thursday

OCTOBER

13) Friday

14) Saturday

15) Sunday

16) Monday

OCTOBER

17) Tuesday

18) Wednesday

19) Thursday

20) Friday

OCTOBER

21)	Saturday
22)	Sunday
23)	Monday
24)	Tuesday

OCTOBER

25)	Wednesday
26)	Thursday
27)	Friday
28)	Saturday

OCTOBER

29)	Sunday

30)	Monday

31)	Tuesday

Your Notes

....
....
....
....
....

Traditional massed design is still very popular within so many floral clubs and in large displays. The skill of technique and direction in flower and foliage placements takes many years to perfect, but as seen in the above it can be done. Also seen are two colour separations which add interest to the design.

NOVEMBER

1)	Wednesday
2)	Thursday
3)	Friday
4)	Saturday

NOVEMBER

5)	Sunday
6)	Monday
7)	Tuesday
8)	Wednesday

NOVEMBER

9)	Thursday
10)	Friday
11)	Saturday
12)	Sunday

NOVEMBER

13) Monday

14) Tuesday

15) Wednesday

16) Thursday

NOVEMBER

17) Friday
18) Saturday
19) Sunday
20) Monday

NOVEMBER

21) Tuesday

22) Wednesday

23) Thursday

24) Friday

NOVEMBER

25) Saturday

26) Sunday

27) Monday

28) Tuesday

NOVEMBER

29)	Wednesday
30)	Thursday

Your Notes

....
....
....
....
....
....
....
....
....
....

Horizontal designs are always popular for formal dinners and other celebrations. They are subtle yet have a presence in many formal ceremonies.

When being created, the designer needs to remember the place or position of the design within the surroundings of the venue.

DECEMBER

1)	Friday
2)	Saturday
3)	Sunday
4)	Monday

DECEMBER

5)	Tuesday
6)	Wednesday
7)	Thursday
8)	Friday

DECEMBER

9) Saturday

10) Sunday

11) Monday

12) Tuesday

DECEMBER

13)	Wednesday
14)	Thursday
15)	Friday
16)	Saturday

DECEMBER

17)	Sunday

18)	Monday

19)	Tuesday

20)	Wednesday

DECEMBER

21)	Thursday

22)	Friday

23)	Saturday

24)	Sunday

DECEMBER

25)	Monday
26)	Tuesday
27)	Wednesday
28)	Thursday

DECEMBER

29)	Friday

30)	Saturday

31)	Sunday

Your Notes

....
....
....
....
....

Your Notes

The traditional posy bowl of flowers is always popular, there are many variations on a theme including using all flowers and no foliage, to using just different coloured foliage, rather than flowers, within the colour theme you are working with.

Other Books That May Interest You
Available Online
www.how2books.com.au

JUST RELEASED, 'The Magic of Chelsea' - A Flower Show like no other, 2024.

With over 260, colour photographs, this book is the perfect gift for you or for someone you love. The book features floristry designs created by some of the world's leading designers, a range of new flower varieties, and other interesting topics.

The first release of our 'Magic of Chelsea' Diary. The diary includes some of the flower arrangements shown at this year's show, but it also includes other interesting 'snip it' information.

And, now, we are producing our book calendar which is a handy asset for any body as they sit at their desk working.

And for those people on the move, please don't forget about our new notebook, it's handbag size of A5, so it will fit into any bag.

The book, 'How To Create Easy Wedding Bouquets', introduces you to many techniques in wedding bouquet construction, the different methods used to wire different flowers and leaves, how to tape, ribboning the wedding bouquet handle, how to make a corsage, buttonhole and other industry techniques that will start you on a floristry career.

Our education company, Full Potential Education And Training has been developed to support people who want to learn how to build skills for the floristry industry. The course is a CPD Accredited 20-week online course in commercial floristry wedding bouquet making. It has been designed to support people who want to work for themselves and start a business or for those people who want a trade career in the floristry industry. For more information, please email, admin@fullpotentialtraining.com.au

The book, 'How To Create Easy Flower Arrangements', is an introduction to floral art and commercial floristry in flower arranging. The book is designed to help those people who want to learn flower arranging and construction techniques and will give the foundation knowledge to those people who want to work in the floristry industry.

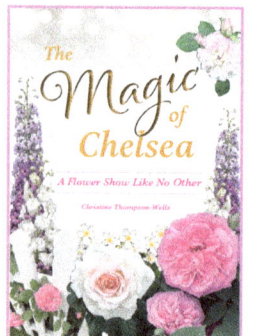

It will also help people who want to learn flower arranging for pleasure and gift giving, and those people who create flower arrangements for special occasions.he Magic of Chelsea, 2022, is full of information covering the Chelsea Flower Show, floristry, art and design, sculpture, different plants and how they are used and has other informative and relevant information that gives the reader different information about the topics included. It would be an ideal book for florists, garden centres, nurseries and like businesses to have as a book for sale in their business. For wholesale information, please email: admin@booksforreadingonline.com

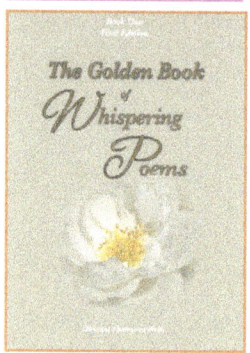

Because we love the books we create, and poetry is a big part of the work we do, we could not help ourselves but include this book of different poetry.

Without plants, we cannot survive. As all flower and lovers know, many plants and trees are under threat! Plants not only help to keep our planet and wildlife healthy, but they also add to our human wellbeing.

This book outlines the benefits of using herbs in our everyday lives. It is colourful and gives a breakdown of herb uses.

www.ingramcontent.com/pod-product-compliance
Lightning Source LLC
Chambersburg PA
CBHW051538010526
44107CB00064B/2775